THE GOODBYE TOWN

THE GOODBYE TOWN

Timothy O'Keefe

Oberlin College Press
Oberlin, Ohio

The FIELD Poetry Series, vol. 26
Oberlin College Press, 50 N. Professor Street, Oberlin, OH 44074
www.oberlin.edu/ocpress

Cover and book design: Steve Farkas
Cover art: Kurt Schwitters, "Merz 1926, 12. Little Seamen's Home"
© 2010 Artists Rights Society (ARS), New York / VG Bild-Kunst, Bonn

Library of Congress Cataloging-in-Publication Data

O'Keefe, Timothy, 1979-
The goodbye town / Timothy O'Keefe.
    p. cm. — (The FIELD poetry series ; v. 26)
ISBN-13: 978-0-932440-40-2 (alk. paper)
ISBN-10: 0-932440-40-1 (alk. paper)
I. Title.
PS3615.K46G66 2011
811'.6—dc22
                        2010046632

Contents

There is a great fig tree grows there, dense with foliage, and under this shining Charybdis sucks down the black water. For three times a day she flows it up, and three times she sucks it terribly down; may you not be there when she sucks down water, for not even the Earthshaker could rescue you out of that evil.

—Homer, from *The Odyssey*

The leaves of the sea are shaken and shaken.
There was a tree that was a father,
We sat beneath it and sang our songs.

—Wallace Stevens, from "Variations on a Summer Day"

Candle

Wick, flicker in. Make
a limpid heap of us.
Spark the chandelier, pour
its chilly prisms.
The wall has always
wanted you, wanted
a slender face.
The plate will cradle
your slow vein, O
do, do
we won't peek.
The vents will fluff
your blue-trim dress
when we pull the shade.
Let up, let up
your tiny braid.
Skim the nooks—
we're here—
ply the light
yes, like that.
There's a shy puppet
in us. Lean in—
we'll show our black pins.

And Styx Was a Children's Book

A flotilla tricks the river silver:
no asking what riffles the water
no *walk an inch in their shoes*
no cemetery songs.

Look: an inksop comic book, a rubber duck
for blustery afternoons:
red leaf, red cheek running
near a forgotten sea.
We woke and the sea had been
a valentine, cardinal song, the maples
stripped bare again. Look: the Chia Pet we
imagined warm when father ran the tub.
Lemon tile for light, smooth shampoo, and oh
lucky duck: yellowest yellow against the open bill.

Broken Sonnet
Dinner Bell

Men fought
and their wives were steeped in applejack.
The butcher's hours were 2-5 AM,
when hospital moms zombied in
with semblances
of a girlish smile.
We learned to track
time
in the rusted row of Pontiacs
on yet another lot.
At 3 PM, the shops closed,
traffic snaked on Highway 10,
and the butcher sniffed a heap of babybacks.

So yeah, I wanted
up
and quick. I'd heard
the single mill sing in its singular stink.
My mother flayed the fat,
tenderized a chewy cut of meat.
A starlane purred, the dealer shook another hand, and I'd think
This is the time for hatchlings.
Time for flies.

Birth Certificate: A. F. Little

Miles up and off, a thousand metal holds
drop their bombs, pock
a cumulus womb.
The sun is its own diorama:
Char bird. Sky shell.

A helmet twitches in a trench.
Things fold from above like marionettes.
The hills blush mustard.
Tanks camouflage a white beach.

In a new suburban hospital, light is striped like a breath mint.

Little wriggles through his deaf tunnel,
first reversal: the flak frizzles. Warheads

scream (before arrival)

in the amniotic seal
of his newly opened mouth.

Broken Sonnet
The Letting

The body withholds. It's not
its fault. We steer it, give it a name, a place
to sleep, to shake. A train
needles the woods. The city lake
is sutured blue. The way a thought
endears itself to the thinker—that's the way
it bears its name,
the body. It gives
what it won't take:
itself, whether we're toweling off
or raking leaves, there's always more
to be shed. We cheer it up:
a bowl of figs, a wooey nocturne,
a snowball snow, a snow
just passing through. It's
not our fault. The things we hold are
not us. There
there—the way a summery time
keeps turning on
itself, turning its edge
in you, the body's edge—
the X inside its spot.

Simmer

Bells in the alley,
wind in the bells,
& Little can't remember
which boot to untie first.
The kettle's on, the radio, Alban—
the neighbor's boy that never grows—
salting the walk. Boots
are cold at first.
The air is cold,
like wind,
when you take them off.

Little splays in a rocker.
The highway's on, a clock
wound elsewhere. Separate sounds
to separate what's near, a shiver,
the smallest hairs on the ear.

Car-noise & sun-noise.
The heel-to-toe voyages repeat, pass, repeat.
Little steeps his chamomile.
How now he says a bit funnily. *How now*
like a cathedral, a boy's voice,
the greengrape spring.

Love

A clear-gold cicada shell
hooked hard to wet bark.
Center-split: antennal
to lower thorax. Molt-clean.

Remember
its clutch in the dark.
Remember

a body-peek green.
A droning wind-hinge.
A fingerful of sudden wings.

Meditation in Red, Blue, and Violet

The highway counts miles from where
we left a transistor radio, a bowl of fruit,
dusk. We talk about the way things fit.
Red : White. Sun : Sky.
Red : White. Strawberry : Seed.
We talk about the sadness of an eclipse.

We wave hellos, goodbyes:
San Clemente, Sun City, Twentynine Palms, Big River.
Someone will call. No one will answer.
A little cough whenever our voices
are speaking there: *Hi, no one's here right now...*

Of course, there will be rumors in town:
figures at an infant's crib,
dog carcasses in a ring of stones,
worms in the apple harvest—
all of which will point to us.
This is how the brain compensates
for emptiness. We're kept alive
by the spaces we've fled
like the reversed ridge of a spine
in the couch cushions.
Like the afternoon I watched
a storm run into the gulf.
Brackish folds flared in the wake and I thought
turquoise, royal, midnight.
I saw the sand, all of it.
The sand held the shape of my legs.

At an all-night rest stop
we piss and fill up.

We sip bad coffee (a little cough).
The radio says weather's bad
in the places we're headed.
The parking lot stirs
red brake, blue moon
and I think of starting up again,
your hand finding my thigh—
lavender, violet, plum.
It's microscopic really,
but with the windshield's short distance
I can block a star in a single breath.
I can feel the car seat that,
empty,
I'd somehow kept warm.

Poem in a Book That Was Never Opened

The wind is giving, giving,
taking. Red maple, red maple,
sun of a sunless root.
There was a home.
We called it *here*.
The big lamps burned
and the wind was humming
then: taking, taking,
giving red
maple, red maple.

The branches wave a shape of air:
the wind is there and here's
a can that clanks along the street, the tin
rush of soldiers' feet.

We'll say
the shapes are not bereaved of weight.
We said
the town is not besieged.

Broken Sonnet
Covenants

You like the top.
You grapple over me.
Things trickle down: a briny bead, a curl,
your sound. The interlace of
flex: a girl with violets, bon voyage, and honeybee.
I never feel
the way you slide
a tee shirt beneath my head.
I like to watch
a twirl of headlights cross the wall—
I'm pressed like a pearl.
You like the top.
You like to bury me.

Midnight is streaked
with owls unlocking fields.
A boy whistles
across a parking lot.
The river looks
for something good to eat.

We speak of covenants. The way to yield, capitulate.

We love us
We love us not
tonight.
Don't slip.
Don't think
I'm incomplete.

If Aeneas

The trouble with memory
is that it's always
today. The bus windows fill—
a boy in white galoshes, a stream
of brick, a see-through face
behind me—with pushy visions.
Perhaps the boy is bluesy
with welts, the way an undertaker whistles
and drains a bloated leg.
They happen all day—
the arrivals that never quite do.
A cup runneth over
where potholes grace the street.
A wife dies on Thursday
when *The Sea Horse* serves a watery margarita
and for this reason, today is always
rimmed with salt.

Rain is a proper shade—day of smoke,
the boy's limp, the stream punctured with trees—
for the woman that slides next to me
looking exactly the way
I need her to look.

Little Arithmetic

1,
She suns on a hill,
all the field becoming
its color, horizon
what she cannot feel
but aligned, lighting
the North Pole northerly.
A green wind winds
shoal to shoal, fallow coast, and spring
piecemealing Spring, sewing leaves
on a white camisole.

2,
She and he and the lake are
mostly water. Look—she won't
take his shrug as such-and-such
a sign—red pouring, pining for.
A canoe, skinny trees as far
as the eye projects
summer spaces.
She and he and water are
the color of whatever holds them.

3,
The leaves are down, the leaves.
The forest blows a window, a waiting-to-be.
She thinks in red-green. He thinks *brown, brown, brown.*

Broken Sonnet

It's a Wonderful Life

If Bedford Falls is
a chrysalis of hanging Christmas lights—
the bleed-up, all in one:
a tie-dye knot, a wish—then my life
was sprung from a tinfoil star
and Jimmy Stewart's twang.
I still recall the hymn
my father sang as he lay in bed:
low oooos, melodic runs,
a hollow in the wall
where his voice
hung then
dawn floating
like a ribboned boomerang.

How then, can a cozy name
betray our need for something
ultrahuman, polychrome?
We pause on bridges, beaches, daisied hills
as if Jimmy were kissing Donna Reed,
but the satellites
are never coming home. We live
in peek-a-boo stars.
In afterthrills.

Alban

No papier mâché sunglasses.
No stars stuck to ceilings.
No bunk beds.

A street with a nerve ending:
the 200-watt house,
too few windows.

The everyday it takes
for Little to pass it by.

Static-air Tuesday, the blinds
have eyes. Cruel
Wednesday's machine.

No Jell-O before supper.
No Jell-O after supper.
Parched yard.
Barren blueberry bush.
Leftovers.

Little found the fig tree, no figs,
the plastic egg with German coins.
He took it, took himself & watchfully, but no

tricycling today not today.

Bell and basket.
Handlebarred mud,
spokeless. A week

and Little checks the tenuous space:
a boy echoes his empty:
maroon, a second egg.

Broken Sonnet
Girlfriend

Morning is not for heroes
or a nine-year-old with sweaty palms.
I hear the hush of slippers in the hall,
the toilet-flush, my father's
heels on the stairs. A shadow
signs against the door—dewdrop limbs,
veiny vines, and something tingling—me
in a tree. Blush and bramble.
I tiptoe, ease the knob, and push
into my father's room. She's there—an outline

I can touch. Curved like a breeze.
The sheets are white but also not.
Somehow, I'm how
the bedposts creak, why
her shins scratch my feet.

It hurts—the way
a pine wants climbing.

Now she slides my hands
beneath the sheets. I'm where
the language ends—
my father's toes on the stairs.

Little Understanding

Sergeant Little's head is a winter fur, a frost,
a single shriveled pupa. On his midnight walk he sometimes
confuses the moon for an eyeless, toothless face
fluttering over the nunnery.

John the Butcher thinks he saw the doubled sun
of Little's bifocals in the window
as he glazed a Peking duck.

Alban wheels toward the chess club
where vets sip from stolid mugs, say
never heard the name.

Little teases the angle of his bathroom mirror,
swings it, watches a face sneak by.
He fingercombs his beard,
touches his cheek as if to cover a hole
or to trigger the handsome lips he wore:
some mauve-and-butterflied space of youth
now soured with rye, a humdrum faith,
an abscessed tooth.

If Scylla

A root swells.
A slab of sidewalk nicks a toe. Then

a slack handshake
a chatty waiter
a pyre lighting the lake
and who doesn't feel

my puppy voice? The urge
to kill a man
is a moth in a paper mouth—nothing,
I say, can fly from here.

The bay is throatless.
The bay is wellwater.
My boats, my boats, my little toy boats.

The urge to kill a man
is a fresh broom in the forest.

Little's Unforgetting, Part 1

Bright as pigeons pixeling the city sky.
Aqua collars and plume. Lavenders lace
the air-break between. Then high careen
and half-bloom. A low-down tug at the tethers.

Sullen Little hunched over a sewer grate.
No photo. Just a pecking backwashed face.

An Absolute Motion, Now We Are Going

If she should turn the corner—

      shanty copper   copper freeze
          sodden paper alleys

—turn quickly
into recognition.

Image this & thereafter: steeple   gutter   sack of oranges

The lighthouse lights, has no keeper.
That way our thumbs release the fragrant peel
and a ship turns every which way
into sea.

Broken Sonnet
Condensation

I might have said that skin
was its own ark (I said
such things), but the curtain never
would be clear enough
to see through. I guess
I could've worn your bathrobe more
or learned which scars you'd never touch.

When the mirror's edge was sharp
with rust, when the toothpaste
pressed to the wrong end of the tube
it was just like you
to notice.
Then, a blizzard. Then,
you dreamt equations to chart
the numbing: burn = burn.
I guess it should—
like a white flame in snow, a truer smoke.

You sulked for April and all
its trembly green.
I slept in the city's brick soliloquy.

A whole day
we spoke in yups and okeydokes.
The steam cleared:
a sign, a warp, the clinging wood.

If Sirens

Little missed the appointed time
for sweeping tangos, Bordeaux, the derby tilted just
so the face shades. And so,

Alban pedals the same imperfect circle.

The town is nothing
if not inheritance.

The squalls come
dune to overpass to tulip-lined park
where all the statuary are women.
They brood and shine accordingly.
Their only wish is to protect us, some say.
Some say they wait for us
to close our eyes for good.

Alban rings a tinny bell.
The Lutheran choir closes the bake sale.

Weather is the fugal answer
we were watching for.
Simple weather.
A hymn we must enter, enter fully,
or escape.

Little just sits there.

Broken Sonnet

Lost Epilogue

And so the ramparts cuddled with the dirt. The mountain hid its jag in the cool hue of forget-me-not. The shipmates waved *adieu, adieu,* as a rainbow stained the empty berth. The children learn to say *for what it's worth…* The fathers watch the tides, say *howdy do?,* and sleep in their boots. The mothers—well, they knew it'd be like this. (The tide lowers its skirt.) A life that's always coming after, viewed in a fisheye lens: The center lies inert. The edges stretch away. A storm is flirting with the gulls, an artifice of blue bullies the sky, and the children are almost through with learning *it doesn't hurt, it doesn't hurt…*

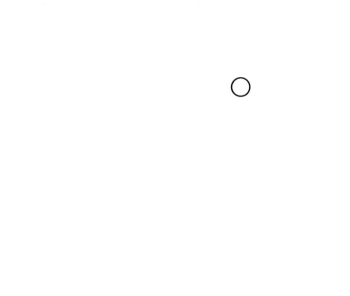

The Outlying Counties and Then Some

Everyone had a mother then, a working train set,
and a nearby promenade to daze among flowers
whose names were difficult to pronounce.
The sun was turning as we turned, though we couldn't see
either very well and the sky held its grayed-in glass (unbreakable),
waiting for the steam to settle, what little talc clings to the neck.
We were talking about the smells of the flowers,
how they never seemed right for the specific time of day,
how the ladies who brought them in wicker baskets
and never said so much as *mornin' honey* or *hi there sweetheart*
made you flush with a homespun affection that only seemed to exist
on the radio, in mahogany voices. Summer didn't last forever,
as many said it wouldn't, and despite the children selecting less colorful
    pajamas,
we could still rely on a few stick-bearers to find that patch of wet cement.

So why this quaking in the trees, the winter sidewalks so quick to melt?
We were circumspect and felt every reason to be: some background
of the thoughts we thought then, laden with parasols or pea coats,
a clean bordering on magisterial that we had acknowledged years before
(we were conscious of doing so) made the rabbits tamer, the squirrels
vaguely harmonious. So much for the rapture of wheatfields, the ones
far enough out we'd have to pack a thermos and several spare tires
before the arrival on a scene of sparse trees, sparsely situated
in a forgiven landscape, the landscape itself a reflection
of the grace that gathered elsewhere. This was, of course,
long before the shortening of salutations,
mauve to midnight and slowly back again,
long before any of us could remember.

Little Crow

The houses are blank tonight,
the windows deep. A pierced kite
filters wind through a pine tree.
The moon's pale debris ignites

dewdrops in a yellow yard.
A screen door snaps like a shard
of night itself. A crow caws
to its straw-stuffed men, regards

the scene with a kind of joy:
prodigal, wide as a boy
in a sealed crib. The world is
flawless. His. Spun like a toy.

Elegy in Late Spring

The sheriff tells me not to touch
her mouth. There might be evidence
between her teeth, needling the gums.
He waits for me to say goodbye
to a fractured wrist, the berry-swell
where knuckles pressed her neck,
the gelid spill where someone yanked
her pigtails up: a lickerish kiss,
and down: an eggshell skull, cement.
I nod. They zip her up in black.

My father had said *You shouldn't chase*
your sister through the streets. She's scared
of playing freeze-tag after dark.
But I kept it up: the game where she learned
a scream so loud it couldn't come out,
the way a body petrified.

I threaded her through the lilac night
as if my hand would be the last
to touch her hair. As if my teeth
could never flash in a stranger's mouth.

Little's Unforgetting, Part 2

A song begins on the other
side of a wall, near ordinary leaves.
A dog yelps punctually.
Bushes toss their birds.
Three months, a winter's nap,
and you could say he's acquired
a sultry hum, a way of making things
fluid in themselves.
He's learned to play
a cowbell heroically, an oboe
that loses children at sea.
She never believed in such bleak whimsies,
despite the altos coughing
roses from the balustrade.
He still takes his evening walk
through multiple time signatures.
His precious jokes are preciouser—
the last raccoon to leave the barrel.
A song on the other side
of a wall begins. He begins.
That smell of brine begins
so many islands from here.

If Palinurus

You put me here.

Where ships are small
and darkly elegant. Where high
currents lace opaque.

I probe a craggy floor
for clues. Opal coral,
the anemones wooing

lugubrious forms.
On the verge of *waken*,
they lid with prickly fish.

I weigh less than a buoy
but you've tethered me far below
blue. I despise your epiphanies

and still the bubbles rise.
I nuzzle a reef's algae collar
and when a mythic squid drifts by

I reach for the salt blonde tentacles.
They wave and wave away.
The gods love a tormentor.

I remember day like a first word,
then sleep tugging
a thousand meters down. Look

up. Say something.
Let me hear the sound
of my celestial chain.

Now Means They Once Were Otherwise

She comes in
a weapon of choice.
She gives in
but not to him.
She presses her

six feathers
the snow-long shore
jetty crush

and she is gone.

She is an empty robe.
She is a candy ring.

Little flits fingers in the dark:
A planet's orbit, closing.
A small, innumerable feast.

Obituary Penciled on a Piece of Drywall Along Highway 55

Something moaned from under the kitchen linoleum. We couldn't say how long it huddled there. The TV had been left on. The kids had been screaming or laughing. Weeks passed. It grew louder when we did and stayed loud as we did. It was a drafty time. After a night of fisting or loving, the bedroom carpet would hold a blistering liquid. We kept on and on. One day it was so quiet. We embraced like straight men and said *dead!* And who can help himself? You peered into the crawl-space. Crept in. Poked over the muscles, mouth, and eyes. *What do you see?* I asked. Your last words were: *My. Opening. Alive.*

Broken Sonnet
Our Own Rumpelstiltskin

The storytimes were buoyant as far
as those things go. We never dragged
our only cow to market or found
a Jolly Rancher house (fluorescent
smoke curling from a Pez-rowed
chimney) or gasped at the squeaky man
who chose our first born.
And we never questioned how
a few beans could unearth the sky.
Our vows of fiction reigned.
In them, we learned the lows

from the lowers. Maybe, behind the scenes, Jack did
things and should've been devoured with Hansel too.
Those things we did
to sleep, wake up,
and pour our bowls of Cheerios.

That sun was a lid
to somewhere else.
We couldn't look
or knew not to.

We wanted names.
We watched the floor.

The Figurine Is Tipped Over

Little languishes in yellow windows along the square.
Winter presides in a windy cloak.
Step. Step. A jet overhead:
snow-sounds.

The Kay-Bee display
holds soldiers in bunkers
that keep holding. The soldiers hold
the line that Little—
without scented letters or Greta Garbo playing cards—
holds for them:
Each toy seems prologue to some great amiss.
One lies belly-up. *Belly-*
open. Another steadies the muzzle
in his mouth. Click. Click:

puddle-sounds.
Little worries the squeak, a soldier's plastic feet.
And let him ply his music. Heavy-heeled
his shadow doubles in the street.
One erases the other.

Whish. *Wish.*
It does no good:
the sound of something stuck in a gutter.

The Corner of She and He

She hit him.
The dog ears lifted, then dropped.

He thought of clenched eyelids, thunder.
He thought of faces at the fire pit.

Black tires smeared the black street.
The windshield webbed then threw him.

She thought of flowers flinching in the dark.
She thought of her husband's folding hands.

The sternum cracked against a curb.
Ribs, lung.

She thought of owls hooing from high boughs.
She thought of lobsters clawing the pot.

The mouth crooked open, stayed that way.
Blood funneled over tongue and teeth.

He thought of his mother washing apples.
He thought of hammocks sagging in the shade.

Broken Sonnet

It Begins in Black and White

Don't say my photo doesn't rearrange
itself to match your
mood. A sepia square, bleached at the edge,
obscures a circling pair
of crows—the way my smile unhooks like a hinge.
Don't say my mustache never tickled
your binge of me.
Don't curse the hole in my copper
stare. Our always-here was always really
there: impressionistic, a night-
pixeled change.

The moon is dropsical. The dogwoods swoon
as if their rings were coming loose.
A caw alerts
the wheatfield's mice—the way a sigh can stretch the sky
thin as a used balloon.
A storm becomes the coast.
Our tides redraw the land.
You said *like darkrooms*
where nothing dries.

Star, Toboggan

Limber is close enough to *lumber* kind of
like *zinfandel* and *hatchet*. Or so

Ashbery said, but inexactly, Ashbery
being Ashbery, and wasn't that

the point all along? We cannot really say
otherwise—though the day wears us

almost fashionably, pilled or pulled each
according to this billowed firmament,

this falling mountain, this tea-lit supper.
I know you know what I wanted

to mean. I gave thanks
for the gumdrop you offered me

once, following the pesto pizza
that took all afternoon to make

and twenty minutes to eat.
We wiped the table, lounged on the patio,

and you said *Well that was all delicious.*
Yup I said, brushing crumbs from my lap.

It was autumn, balmier than we'd expected
and the pines made their ritual gestures

not to each other, though salutatory,
but to that which could not wave back.

All that I said *and that, and that.*

Why I'm Not Photogenic

The cruelest part of me is just inside my right eye:
petal-red, invisible.

This is our concession, our nightly Polaroid.
You always catch my turnaways.
I never let you see me
watching you brush your hair.

There's an overfocus, a submersion:
today a store window ogles me. I turn
and mannequins start undressing.
Tomorrow's rearview runs a world away.

Last night I saw you in the bedroom mirror
watching me. You tried to reach. You turned
and slid your jeans back on.
The moon was a boutonnière

on the mirror, in the mirror,

we pinned like a blind spot.
So many moons we wore:
sphere or sickle, radiant, magnanimous,
and we couldn't bear to look.

Broken Sonnet
Grief

The door scrapes. No one says
a sound. A box of hushed lips
in the bedless master suite.
Or rats inside the walls.
The unknown meat
of night. *The waves...* she said.
No ticks, just tocks.
Wind grass dirt worms and the dead
like empty docks. *I used to be so gutless* she'd repeat.
No more. You could say
I'm in the driver's seat.
The awful calm of a ship inside the locks.

That door again. It isn't me. What's
here? The fruit's piled up inside the bowl
and bruising.
The clothesline whips its sleeves.
Relents in the rain. That's that. I'm going
to stay.
...the captain steers.
I think of me. The world. The things
we're losing. Our made-up word for
please no not again

Figures from a Clairvoyant Time

Couples carlights
quicken citrus
November night.

Scissor-a-step
each in   each
pond apple
macula.

Elsewhere they
who are thistle-borne
prelude   winter

in white.
Westerly westerly
blizzard sheen

pond   for walking
                              eye-
in-ear   imbricate   wind-
sphere—tender
a hidden stitch.

A stalk for miles
years of miles
crêpemoon sea.

Bristle forth
thy spiracles
heaving   immaculate:

so blue thy evergreen.

Broken Sonnet

It Ends in Black and White

How to remember what I couldn't say:
night penciling the clouds to coal the coal to night
and it's fine by me to tip my bowler hat
it's fine by me to run or *stay five minutes* so
I run. The traffic's gray. The horns smoothing. A helicopter
tolling slate. White windows. Tunnel-tones. The scrolled-
up stars. It's fine. One way
is still a way.

You didn't speak.
My hands were in the sink.
I was rinsing coffee spoons.
My hair was penciled up.
My tank top was black
and I blew a strand of hair from my face.
I dropped a spoon.
It clinked.
You didn't speak
so I hummed in my soft bland way
and my tank top was damp.
It was blacker then.

Poem with Contrails

June's last maidens, strolling daybreak.
Tulip-prim, tenor wind
in the flue. The air expanding then: my mother
small along the water.

Who knew the month, the friendly weather?
I was thinking somewhere else so
I was here. *Stray maidens, stay.*
Pray for all my other times of year.

Chimney crumble, bright brick.

Mother and flowers flying and clear.

A plane raking its own snow.

Broken Sonnet
Postpartum

There were no words
for slow explosion,
clowns in a wagon,
kicked awake. Open
the door. Wintering wind
in the screen.
A canker sore.
A porch light turning on or through or down
my thighs. A stretch
of hallways. A riot town. There are
no words.

The ankle-swell
is more than I can miss.
I cry in grocery stores.
The heads of cabbage
purpleface, whitefrown,
and the radishes
have lost their cheeks.
They lie like clots,
the little bulbs.
They blush.
But nothing comes from them,
nothing comes.

The clerk at *Hi-Ho Liquors*
remembers me
most days I'm
sloughing words
for a change.
My voice stays thin.
It's the same as what defines:
They come from us.
They came.

Another Thing That Flies

Little shakes his tail
feathers to a brass parade
sunning up the street. Trumpets
flare up, French horns
mellow-bell, trombones
roll their oiled sleeves.
Little's mouth moves like a beak.

There are only bats at night,
in plum space. Call it
sky. Call it jagged flight:
fingers and valves,
Alban pinching a gummy-worm.

Noon is glossy as a barbershop.
Red stripe, blue stripe,
a cloud of talc, a cloud
without birds when birds
are everywhere else. Call it
a crescendo. Call it Little, flapping
through the eye of a storm.

Broken Sonnet
If Dido

Seahold and broil bequeath…
Our bookend gulls.

*

Who am I when I'm falling in

no, through.

*

The ivy tips its vein across the house.
Green in lightloss, these shades
I keep from you.

*

A song, the words you know you
know the in
-song.

*

Death like some first day all
the banks had lollipops.

*

We were ten and locked in the art
supply room we found the switch
flicked it six-packed acrylics scraggly
brush-heads easel splints fractured
O dovetail vision it was the start

of something red a point
-blank rush a
fix.

*

My ——,
fleetcross white, gone
the pyre's reach.

The Water and Web Variations

I pull at the ancient mangroves. Water and web.
Diction: serrate, dragonfly, lotus. Tone: demoned water, web-
    throw.

Every clink along the shoreline. Pick it up. Keepsake web in
    water.
So much underwatered, undertowed. A tidal cage. Crab-leg
    the phantom web.

A couple fucks on the ferris wheel. Water-tank below. Cotton
    candy webs.
A clown squirts a plastic water-flower. Backdrop: horror-house
    webbing.

Without Web nothing sticks. Water drops its quiet diamonds.
Without Water nothing blooms. Web-wilt the fat cocoon.

No one knocks on the widow's door. Curled floorboards.
    Cobwebs in waterglasses.
The day she died the dahlias were overwatered. The bedroom
    mirror webbed.

My neighbor wants to be an astronaut. We play games. I say
    waterweb.
She says *Saturn's rings* or at times *the universe*. She says *life*. I
    say *waterier, webless*.

I strike a match. All the bush burning. Web and water.
Diction: spiders unspindled. Web-tone: ripple-bright, silk to
    silk, water is a grid.

Little's Unforgetting, Part 3 (A Lynching)

Sleep with me
by a hush-hush
sea. Glance
sprung, chance
slung—
prance around the cherry tree.

It's dark so
sway with me.
My leaflorn song
my neverlong
my mouth in yours—
fill and filler.
We are made
such as this.
Night is
the same touch of burgundy.

Little's First Symptom (The Clawfoot Poem)

Tub tub   boy big

scrubsud   curlicue

boo   wet swirl   blue

soak room   float ring

taffy color soaps

wash today wash away

year   year   g'night dear

carrot   head   tremor boat

Elegy, Aphasia

Colored-in

dawn, a meeting

place between

what we feel

before it's how

we remember.

Color in

some next dawn

orchestral and willing

any color please any

your speaking hand. How

it stencils the air.

Eye/Ear

The fields of Lancaster

Awake in lavender, tilling

Motions in a low sky:

What goes from tree to somewhere

Tree, what runs beneath

A buried bridge.

At a far enough distance, everything

Silent, silent is. Leaf-smear

The train window, Amish girls

Singing in a silo & I

Once heard a buzz saw sunk

In an ocean my

Eyes were full cups closing

In the sound—thinnest blade—

Ears opening for all

That circle-green sea.

Little's Second Symptom

Things rise
sky-notched
and are risen.
A balloon. A tiny hand
still reaching.
Belt of heaven.

In the whereabouts of dread,
we rose to meet
in leaky houses
in doorways
in too-tight clothes.

Things rise
and are risen
toward.
A hand reaching for its clothes.
The dread of doorways.
The air-tight heavens.

We met in the notch of a belt.
The sky leaked through.
The house distilled its air.
We rose in the whereabouts
of tiny balloons.

Another Legend to Tuck Us In

Elms are
elming above eaves

and all the attic
windows lit.

Passers-by loosen
a rope-colored mist.

Wind and wheeze
alert, a-sky,

sleep by sleep O
harm us not.

A doily that never moves,
keyholes leaking music

and all the windowed foliage
wounded, mute.

In days of lost brass keys
a peasant girl dropped

a single white lily

down an abandoned well.
There, she dreamed, by

and by, where all the evening
gowns hung beckoningly.

When We Saw Always & Sudden

These hills are not
like teeth, even
in snow. Especially…

It is summer
so many times over.

The floral horizon
may ribbon, may lip-curve.
My left eye, the steeper, the one
that follows you, unshutters

a thousand tiny telescopes how

can't we find new planets
in every direction, every direction
goodbye.

Trajectory is retrospective & still
there are these hills.
Tree-bleed, lateral light, further & further…

All eyelashes are a desperate color.

Somewhere a knife-row of icicles
melting off, melting in,
blue body blue.

What rings the rivered air.
What stoppers.

Is there rest in this?
A wending into nowhere night.
The smallish distance
your shoulders make.

Little Nocturne

Coal in coal, whitesound,

high the track and

fleet. Tinseled

town, wide in sleep.

That tattered moon.

A black sheet

with a hole.

Poem in the Key of Luminarias

A pack of doorways pressing relentless together
so as to form the hall in which I walk toward
famous blackout you.

Outside warms inward, fruit space, dark pit.
The sun lets fall touchlessly. The wicked spring trees

just when you were getting used to.
Solitude foreshortens—each horizon
vacates to a vein and though

summer comes king and curveball
the sturdiest fence is taken by honeysuckle
the air of their breaking
insatiable. Rest assured:

penguins never dream of flying, even in water.

If turquoise, then winsome fish.
We are overfluent in coral days
where each sky is a cake, a birthday cake
because we've candled it so.

Let the infomercials eyelid our sleep.
The furnace has a reliable voice.
The body is full, if nothing else, and still

we open our eyes in the pool.

Autumns were before or after, depending.
The wind will be here when it goes.

You. You pinkshift through. Speak from me
and what the spruces drop their cones to hold.
Speak in a royal night. What wraps us round
is an origin. Night is a guest with shy hands.
We always dress too quickly.

Little's Third Symptom

The wind and the windows are one hollow sound and it's the same apple-orchard dream. A week now the same. Pink Ladies unripen when I reach for them and I keep reaching till everything's high up and green. But it's late. It's always getting there. Getting to the radio blinking. Getting to Tchaikovsky bleeding Rat King. Getting to a puppy in the window. Brindle boxer. Black and amber but more black so the amber stripes are moments when its mother stopped pushing. Reverse brindle then. Pretty thing in a hollow sound. Mom calls and I don't answer then calls again and I do. A playpal has died dangerously or won something and I never found my cowboy hat. We were gypsies until I could prove otherwise. Days before the next duplex were like rerun lives or running-in-place lives that are cozier in a homemade book where the drawings don't quite match the text but the babysitter smiles and moves on. Nights grew many rows of teeth. I had a dog named Stretch near Cincinnati then Stretch Two near Missoula who could see over the fence on four legs and howled when the Riley girls were called to wash up. The youngest had a sunburn that tinged her freckles green. She told me to chase her. I did. Then trees turn November and November again and Easter baskets lose their Cadbury eggs and the Riley dad drives toward the mountain drives toward E and E is for Empty and he's walking now and it's Christmastime with lights in the valley and him in the mountain and that's that with the same miles everywhere. It happens like this. The always getting there. Many times this and I lose count. The night Stretch Two howled a hollow sound I rubbed my eyes in the yard till the lightning bugs lit. Now they're chased away or maybe they just blink less. Many times less. This many times.

Self-Portrait Against Myself

How to separate

what I feel from

what I want in

you to be.

The browning asters.

The aster-

ing.

Broken Sonnet
Diagram in the Fire

There was a story we'd been meaning
to tell you. You who never cared
for endings. Who

lost your hearing on a listless bay, then found it
sluicing cedars. Who
set fire to keepsake dolls

that never said a word.
You said they never would.
A pair of somethings hid

far past the flames, the field. A space unveiled
in every kind of night.
You'd heard enough to know

the dolls made ruddy faces then,
their jackets settling into lacquer.

Clothes clothed,
the unraveled eyes,
the hushings-up:

they're all a part, all orchestrated now, now in voice.

Treetops: Told.
A warning, skin: Told.
Our engulfing smallness: Told.   Told.   Told.

Acknowledgments

Grateful acknowledgment is due to the editors of these publications in which poems or versions thereof have appeared:

American Poetry Review: "Poem in the Key of Luminarias"

Barrow Street: "Obituary Penciled on a Piece of Drywall Along Highway 55"

Blackbird: "Elegy in Late Spring"

Boston Review: "Poem in a Book That Was Never Opened"

Cimarron Review: "Meditation in Red, Blue, and Violet"

Columbia Poetry Review: "Broken Sonnet: Diagram in the Fire" and "Broken Sonnet: It's a Wonderful Life"

Conjunctions: "Elegy, Aphasia," "Eye/Ear," "The Outlying Counties and Then Some," and "Poem with Contrails"

Denver Quarterly: "Little's Unforgetting, Part 1" and "The Water and Web Variations"

Electronic Poetry Review: "Broken Sonnet, Dinner Bell" and "Little Arithmetic"

FIELD: "Another Legend to Tuck Us In," "Broken Sonnet: Our Own Rumpelstiltskin," and "Why I'm Not Photogenic"

Forklift, Ohio: "Little's Second Symptom," "Little's Third Symptom," and "When We Saw Always & Sudden"

Gulf Coast: "Broken Sonnet: The Letting"

Indiana Review: "Broken Sonnet: Postpartum"

Konundrum Engine Literary Review: "If Scylla"

Lo-Ball: "Another Thing That Flies," "Birth Certificate: A. F. Little," and "Simmer"

Mid-American Review: "The Corner of She and He"

New American Writing: "And Styx Was a Children's Book" and "Broken Sonnet: Covenants"

Pleiades: "Broken Sonnet: Grief" and "Broken Sonnet: Lost Epilogue"

Pool: "Broken Sonnet: It Begins in Black and White" and "Broken Sonnet: It Ends in Black and White"
Subtropics: "Candle" and "If Palinurus" (subsequently appeared on *Verse Daily*)
32 Poems: "Love"
Western Humanities Review: "If Aeneas," "Little Nocturne," "Self-Portrait Against Myself," and "Star, Toboggan"

So many necessary thank-yous:

To the University of Utah, the Bread Loaf Writers' Conference, Johns Hopkins University, and the Tin House Writer's Workshop for providing time and space for these poems; to Manuel Toledo, Dan Gutstein, Sean Singer, Dave Smith, Donald Revell, Karen Brennan, Kate Coles, Paisley Rekdal, Craig Dworkin, D. A. Powell, Dean Young, Peter Gizzi, and Susan Howe for their formative influence and generosity; to Geoff Babbitt, Kathryn Cowles, Rebecca Lindenberg, Christine Marshall, Stacy Kidd, Alex Lemon, Julia Delacroix, and Caki Wilkinson for their shrewd counsel and encouragement; and finally, to my friends and families, for their support and love.

"Elegy, Aphasia" is for John Robert Lottes.
"When We Saw Always & Sudden" is for Darcie Dennigan.